D0344753

Also by W. S. Di Piero

Poetry

The First Hour

The Only Dangerous Thing

Early Light

The Dog Star

The Restorers

Shadows Burning

Essays

Memory and Enthusiasm

Out of Eden: Essays on Modern Art

Shooting the Works: On Poetry and Pictures

Translations

Pensieri, by Giacomo Leopardi

The Ellipse: Selected Poems of Leonardo Sinisgalli

This Strange Joy: Selected Poems of Sandro Penna

Ion, by Euripides

Skirts and Slacks

Skirts and Slacks

poems

W. S. Di Piero

ALFRED A. KNOPF

New York   2001

THIS IS A BORZOI BOOK
PUBLISHED BY ALFRED A. KNOPF

www.randomhouse.com/knopf/poetry

Knopf, Borzoi Books and the colophon are
registered trademarks of Random House, Inc.

Grateful acknowledgment is made to the following publications,
where some of the poems in this book previously appeared:
*Afterimage, Chelsea, Literary Imagination, The New Criterion, The New
England Review, The New Yorker, Partisan Review, The Progressive,
Threepenny Review, TriQuarterly* and *The Yale Review.*

ISBN 0-375-41153-4
Library of Congress Control Number: 2001088080

Manufactured in the United States of America
First Edition

For Mary Jane and Daniela

Johann Ernst Burggrav's alchemical book *Lampadem vitae et mortis* describes how to take some of your blood, distill it, and use it to feed a small oil lamp. The lamp will flare up when something good happens in your life and it will gutter when you fall on hard times. The lamp will stay lit as long as you are alive, and when you die, it will go out.

—James Elkins, *What Painting Is*

CONTENTS

ONE

TWO

THREE

ONE

Cheap Gold Flats

1. "PHILLY BABYLON"

The bartender tossing cans, carton to cooler,
hand to hand with silky, mortal ease,
while the 4 p.m. beer and shot standees
study the voiceless TV above our heads.
The worst and longest storm on record.
Iceworks canal the pavements, power lines down,
cars pillowed helpless in the snow.
Bus fumes vulcanize the twilight's
911 sirens. Enter HOTSPUR, with alarums,
enter HAZEL, touching my elbow at the bar.
My staticky *Daily News* breaks in the draft.
"What's my horoscope say today, honey?"
Dear Hazel, dear Pisces, don't be hurt,
leave me alone a while, my mother's dying,
I've been beside her bed for several days,
today she had an extremer monkey look,
her forehead shrunk down to the bucky jaw,
and when she looks above her head, she groans
to see whatever it is she sees, so here,
take my paper, go home, forgive me.

2. FINISHED BASEMENT

Tonight's big question: What will she
be laid out in? Disco tracks
jump inside the paneling.
Rita loved to dance and so do I.
The sisters, Rachel and Jeanette,
and nieces coming straight from work,
shout across her bed, voicing with
our faithful music in the walls.
Charm bracelet, definitely, the one
she hardly wore, and cheap gold flats
that made her look young and men look twice.
Yackety-yak. The unconscious bone
doesn't miss a thing we say,
its used-up flesh helpless
on the pillow. Later, alone with her,
the only noise near me is this new rattle
in her throat. I hear it behind me, too,
the disposal upstairs, a drainpipe clearing,
whatever it is, I feel it coming closer
to finger my hair and stroke my neck.

Psychopomp

Dropsical, juggy, yellowgreen,
like Dante's Master Adam.
Consciousness taffied by drugs
into and out of the dull light
scalding from the bedside lamp,
balled sheets at his big feet,
my father, just before he died,
sat up by his own strength,
uncannily, and seemed then
Dante's other lost soul,
bemused and contemptuous
of the hell in which he lay.
In arrogant wakefulness,
he said: "Pete? Pete?"
Calling to my uncle who,
unheard and unannounced, walked in
a minute later, not knowing
he'd been summoned, or recognized,
by the dying animal which,
having spoken its last words,
now lay back, dimmed,
cracking the pillow. And now
I have to ask (how many times
have I asked already?)
not why you spoke at all,
but how you knew it was Pete,
who once let me touch the scar
that creased his forehead,

where the Nazi bullet punched
his rakish helmet
then skidded up his skull.
Meaning runs so densely
in such things, then,
just as momentously,
there's no meaning at all.
That's what keeps me here,
the pain of those two things.
I want more and more
to go where you once went,
though I don't know where
that is, or if it is.
Such famous last words.

Money

In my uncle's wallet,
among his few remains,
my mother's sister found
a thousand dollars, loose
big bills. She never knew.
And so she spent that week
uncapping jars, cans,
toolbox crannies where
he might have hidden more,
more than the lacquered
nudist magazines
(the kind my father hid
in workshop cabinets)
exhibiting children, parents,
and sunburnt elders.

Two weeks later
another aunt died,
oldest of the four sisters,
born "over there."
I read her books.
The Silver Chalice,
Reader's Digest Condensed,
an abridged *Miserables.*

After church, my mother,
sobbing on the phone,
says we're nothing.
(*Vein, marrow, tendon,*
horn, hair, and thoughts.
These don't matter.)
"We're nothing, us. That's what."

At St. Hubie's Altar

The effort of it, the Egyptian
teenage-princess look.
Crushed cinnabar blush,
the surprised large mouth
her brown lip liner draws,
gelled tresses ribbed
across the runway shoulders,
so many modeling classes
to craft a seeable self,
pencil skirt at sixteen
and high-heeled sandals
that snagged the casket's red
carpet. Tripped toward
the aunt she never liked,
who disliked her because
she never listened to nobody
and acted like she owned
the world, she weirdly seemed
to want to fall inside
and be with that blanched life,
but someone gathered her
and seined her back to us.
How she must hate that visage
in her vanity mirror,
the silly earnest child,
face banged up by tears,
who can't even help herself,
who drools and bites her hair.

Skirts and Slacks

The .32 Special,
its Dutch Masters box,
still in their bedroom
closet, days after
my mother's death,
plus my father's
thirty years ago.
I used to practice
disarming, reloading,
putting it in my mouth
for fun. And so
here it is again,
but (stupid woman,
Great Depression child
scrolling tens and twenties
in macaroni boxes)
loaded, half-cocked.
Oh yes, shoot the burglar
in the closet, the cat
in heat on the fence,
and Calvin Coolidge. She rose,
rammy, close to death,
cocked up in bed
as if pulleyed by heaven,
sometime past midnight.
I was there to watch
her eyes wake for a moment
enraged and hateful toward me.

Bone wooled with slights
of flesh, what certainty
in the body at its end?
And between here and there?
Breath stops, blood fades,
the comic head I'm lifting
from the pillow feels
too merely anatomical
and heavier than before.

Oregon Avenue on a Good Day

Some nights I dream the taste
of pitch and bus fumes and leaf meal
from my old exacting street.
This time home, I'm walking to find

I don't know what. Something always
offers itself while I'm not watching.
I'm hoping for a certain completion,
of housefronts or myself. I don't want

the standard gold of ginkgo leaves,
or weeping cherries, O how beautiful,
but fused presence, a casual fall
of light that strikes and spreads

on enameled aluminum siding, brick,
spangled stonework, fake fieldstone
and clapboard, leftover Santa lights,
casements trimmed in yellow fiberglass,

our common dream of the *all*
and the *only this,* that's exactly
what I can't find. The best of it
is a racy, homely metric unplanned

line to line, building up a scene:
husband and wife inside, plus kids, suppertime,
pine paneling where scratchy exterior light
rises sweetly above a TV voice.

Leaving Bartram's Garden in Southwest Philadelphia

Outside the gate, the scrawny trees look fine.
New-style trolleys squeak down Woodland
past wasted tycoon mansions and body shops.

There's something I wanted to find,
but what? Roses two months from now
on these brambles? The same refinery fires

lashing over the Schuykill? The adult hand
that held mine here so many years ago?
None of this happened. Across Spring Garden Bridge,

zoo elephants clicked past my window—
birds jumped from dust igniting on their backs.
Inside Bartram's house, elephant-eared

cure-all comfrey leaves hung above the hearth.
A redbird gashed the sunned mullioned glass.
I'm in the weave. The brown-brick project softens

in the sun. Stakes in its communal garden catch
seed packets and chip bags blown across the rows.
Tagger signatures surf red and black

across the wall, fearless, dense lines
that conch and muscle so intimately
I can't tell one name from another.

The Apples

The city budget squads have trimmed its hours.
"You can't get in, just go home why don't you."
I couldn't tell how old she was.
Chalky braids crisscrossed her head;
the trenchcoat bunched around her waist
like paper flowers, her bare legs
streaked pink.
She held a net bag, very French,
filled with cans.

It's equinox.
Sycamore leaves bank at curbs
and blip in bike-wheel spokes.
My old library's closed. It's always closed
when I make visits home.
Starlings rake song across the wires.
I used to ride my meaty Schwinn
to this better neighborhood.
"You can't. You can't." She quivered
and chopped the bag against her knee.

Saying that,
I make a mimicry of her.
I learned to do it
in the big, lemony room of floodlit books.
Gg Zz Bb leafed from the walls.
Sky-blue globe. Soiled card catalog.
Robinson Crusoe walked across the room,
studying matter, its provisioning use

and weedy homemade powers: I put my feet
into his splayed prints in the sand,
but when he looked behind, he said
Find your own place, kid. Grow up.

You can't you can't. I lost her
in the splintered Sears and Pep Boys doors
down the block, the lost-lease sales
and recycling bins.
I feel her words, or think I do,
like matter, plasmic and boreal.
A bus diesels from the curb;
leaves chase its wheels.
Noon light
drenching the tall windows
prints images behind the steel mesh:
clouds crossing sky, stone housefronts,
football rising end over end,
sneakers on power lines like skins
of souls fled or stolen.

Equinox. Measure, middle,
I know I know. All I feel is motion
sucking me in its draft.
The middle's a fiction. I dreamed again
I materialize in the big room,
high ceilings, maybe a sky, the walls
all books sickly organized, but among them
the one true book I'll find by accident.

It will occur to my hands, like Crusoe,
near a textbook's see-through images
of the body's solid veins, muscle mass,
bloodworks and nerve draperies.
It's the book I knew I'd find.

I don't want half measures. The season
slides to winter. That thought's complete.
Her voice, too, stands watch,
sits, I mean, with me on the cold steps,
while I kill time
reading the book I brought along.
Ruskin, who loved fireflies and unities,
says that the dragon
who guards the golden apples
never sleeps, he hoards them
in his finny coils,
and his greatest skill is mimicry,
mocking human voices,
calling to us in tones
we recognize, until we believe
he's something or someone else.
Then it's too late.

Words for Song

Mirror and mantel where his father leans,
talking to Mother, both more real
than the electric nothing the boy fears
himself to be, nuclear vacancies

where the self burns into being,
immaterial and yet skin and bone,
the small feet rhizomed from the floor,
the green of leaves, then fingernails.

Hoping to be something real, the boy
speaks words back to his father,
but the larger being cuts through
the stalk of smoke and talks instead

to Mother. Bitter, mildly crazed words
treed in the body of the son's voice
that keeps amassing every day
its trillion colonies of cellular stuff

until he finally becomes a him, this me
writing, invisible, as my flesh was then.
I say *zaftig halation,* unheard,
and swear by it and by the nobody listening.

The Accident

Where the poet Duncan writes
of salmon climbing the fall,
"a spiritual urgency
              at the dark ladders leaping"
the curled hair dropping in my book
              is my father's
tight waves where he stands quiet
in a corner of the dance floor
while my mother's finger curls
swing with the orchestra.
              When he died
and I caught her as she fainted,
the matted ringlets swung
against my neck. A week before,
I'd trimmed his hair and shaved
the shadow from his skull.
              A hair wobbling
on the page after three days' rain
foamed down to keep the ground
greener longer in my garden.
              The iris
will open soon. After the rains,
the sunned compost, where in time
I'll lay the iris,

steams through wild fennel,
          salmon at the fall
climbing the fleshy banks
of rinds, weed, pulp, and shells,
then writhing in the fennel fronds
that bite their essence into my fingers.

White Blouse White Shirt

Snow falls on the boardwalk
    where they never walked that winter,
streetlamps in white boas, surf light
    patching shuttered storefronts.
Where are they? The Ferris wheel
    they once rode looks green.

In this other snapshot
    she wears pedal pushers,
he's in summer whites,
    they swing cigarettes
and hold hands, walking toward me,
    it seems, into breezy life,
where they don't know I'm waiting.
    Now they're renting a rolling chair.
Inside the wicker cowl he says
    "A five-dollar ride, chief."
"It's Chinese, like Charlie Chan."
    Sand buries the sea noise,
resin scents rise from the boards
    into deft sea winds
as they roll past windows larvaed
    with delftware and sable stoles,
licking each other's fingers,
    french fries in paper cones.

When did the boardwalk look like that?
   When was that fresh love?
I stencil red-winged blackbirds
   into the scenes, and lilac
brushing windowpanes, and crocus,
   one garden of one season,
composite, where we look out,
   and between them I become
an hourglass of sand and light
   beside the ocean,
where the sun lets more snow
   fall around our heads.

TWO

My Message Left Next to the Phone

I'll leave this where I know you'll look.
Doing seventy across the bridge, I stared too long
at the sun breaking through steelwork cheaters
and saw stiffened shadows, fan blades
pulsing across the fast black surface.
Sailboats flew under me like paper gulls.
What happened then was this: "figures"
from the trusses stepped like nutcrackers,
hundreds, tall and elegant, sexual shadows
scissored into life, gauds flint-struck
from the half-dark and sunlight and panic.

I felt they'd come for me, all that speed,
come to gather me in their motion,
rushed off the bridge into the green bay
with its white sails and weightless hulls waiting.
I was theirs for the taking. They'd fold me
in their formal motion, rhymed with sea and light,
self-possessed, not really interested in me.
To evaporate in that traffic air
with them, delivered to some place
I never knew before. I made it
to the other end. Next week I'll try again.

Some Voice

Past the silky gondola hulls
arcaded in the boatyard,
we walked that afternoon
to our favorite grubby campo,
empty except for cats
and one plane tree, with bench.
We loved it so much. We walked
just to be there, imagining
sometime we'd spend the night.
The little hotel, its frank lantern,
its dim sign dimmer by day,
we'd remember, just like that.

The tree's patchy shades worked
down your arm as it pointed up,
over there, locating the voice,
its open window, the soprano scales
tipped down to us. All life
is hidden life. Don't believe
everything you hear. To us,
or not to us, her voice fell
into that year, then ten more.

Routine practice doesn't call
to anyone, it simply falls
through footbridges, black hulls,
and plane tree. When we went back,
the singing wasn't there for us.
We take what's given and work
with that. The rest is grace.

Early February the Same

It came and went fast-forward
late-winter dream speed,
the acacia under my window
blooming practically overnight,
fisty yellow flowers
pomped higher toward me
most of all after rain
stooped and shagged its heights.
How many days later
did you stop by, "What's
going on with that tree?"
and I noticed with you:
blossoms mostly blown
icing the patio's concrete
down there. Where was I?
I must not have been looking
or looking too hard to see,
and now its isolations
spring back higher, farther,
branch, leaf, shredded yellow,
freed from the beauty loads,
another season shortened
in and for ourselves.

U F O

Remember the desert's bluish light?
Dawn or late day? We drove long hours
to clarify our love with speedy talk,
road games we rehearsed but didn't play.
The two-lane blacktop swelled toward us
through sage and rabbit brush, while we picked
at recent jealousies, glittery ghosts of fact,
whom you or I would sleep with, whose lips we liked best.

You slept on it. Evening, it must have been.
I kept driving on pills and coffee.
Curled loosely in your seat, you breathed
as you still do, hissing softly,
worn out by lost checkbook or keys.
I imagined someone else's touch on your thigh,
then touched it without waking you.
The stars began to shine outside the windshield.

That's when I saw the round flat lights,
five of them, like star points.
Bright invisible lines locked them in place
until they moved, switched hemispheres,
here, there, hummingbird-style.
I pursued them, trying to catch up
while I shook your leg so you could watch
with me. They waited only until you woke.

You believed what I said, I think,
not in what I'd seen. They were there,
they were not. They saw me
with the same eye with which I saw them.
What I met there, while you slept,
is exactly what I've just said again to you.

At Mission Carmel

Headless serpents, signs of something
or decorative motifs,
fluted forms trenched
into each pillar's edge.
Fired-up roof tiles, mothy timbers,
shade, stone benches margining
the cloister's laddered darks and light.
We knew we'd been there before.

Not there. Bologna, the porticoes,
jalousied depths and curves sliding
in that other life of ours, this life,
that's what we remembered
walking under the mission eaves,
alive in two times at once,
as if we could tell true mystery
from merely ornamental harmonies.

The frilled girl who goose-stepped
on the mission stones
loved the strickenness her patent-leather pumps
called from the ground, like heels
of evening shoppers on Via San Vitale
whose shadows, at different speeds,
cut across the pillars. Chasing them,
we made such figures, too.

Our girl of the Americas led us
to the church doors: a sullen bride
walked down the organ-curdled aisle,
father on her arm, mother behind
to govern the train. We watched it all.
The mission bells tolled. Ten years ago.
Where are you now, love? Do you still hear
the heels of our shadows dancing there?

Vincent van Gogh's
Self-Portrait: 1887

Small and great, like money,
small actions like striking a match,
smiling, moving the candle.
We're hostage to a world of likeness
we also come to love. Like Pat
in the parlor once a week
writing numbers on dimpled foolscap
folded inside his hat
before he took our small-time bets.

He's here again on that postcard
you sent with the latest check,
remodeled into the painter's countenance:
red beard, magmic hat,
cerulean tie rhymed with lapel edging.
(The motif doesn't matter,
what matters is the treatment.)
"Here's the tax money I owe till June."

Unshaven, filthy hatband of Mongolian silk—
today must be somebody's lucky day.
Money, small-time, the painter's work
a daily prayer improvised and of use.
When you and I bought raspberries,

a yellow chair, the hand-painted bowl
with its black thunderbird wings spread
and fading now, a world passed between us
that was gone when you left.
Thanks for the card. Next payment's due in the fall.

Malocchio

Snakebit where there are no snakes,
under a dark cloud in her kitchen,
I explained my problem, that space
assumed weird shapes.

"What kind of shapes?"

Funnels. Cyclonic eggbeaters.
Opening out of me like a bell
whose music I'm forced to be.
My blood spins, too. It's awful,
and I feel weaker by the day.

"Very complicated."

The old lady's toaster gleamed.
On its surface mused her fridge,
stove, and some colored vials.
I explained I couldn't sleep,
had cold sweats, felt confused
by things like that toaster.
She cocked her head at me,
and tapping the corner of her eye
lanced (she said) the evil pouch
someone's look had sewn into my brain.

"You'll be okay now."

O malarial rose-scented love.
Sparrow wings and thorns.
Spiky dewdrops. Fur.

Nipples, juice, breath, pulse.
It didn't work. I still want back
the hand and voice that bit me.

Less Than Two Minutes

When your footpads
wet after a bath
left prints like
our conversations
every which way
in that small house
I couldn't tell
where you went
or in what mood.
Box toes
flat meaty arch and stone
participial bunion
pulled me toward
uncertainty where
I feel most at home
so I followed without
caring which way
I should turn.

Aisle-Seat Soliloquy

I believe what you said
about truth in words,
straight plain talk,
that's all you want.
But the plain style
isn't simple.
It's a fictive face
glazed on the air
between us. It flaps
its lip, speaks kind
or injurious words.
What did I say?
Tray tables and seats
in upright position.
I can't remember
what I said that hurt,
and the jets are wowing.
A coarse laugh rends
the fattened air.
Across the aisle,
a blissy girl
tents her head
with a blanket, chanting,
while the video's
veronica face
barks and reminds me
how tossed you were
by words I can't remember.

Forgive me. Sometimes
I'm unreal to myself.
The bad laugh that broke
behind me sounds like you,
trying to tell me something
although I'm hardly here.

The Skylight

The rain speeds up.
Vague hillsides greener
south of the city,
until today's break.
I walked up my street
past toddlers squealing
over red chalk suns
and green stars.

Take this and that.
The world's peremptory force
adheres to us
and screens us out.
It lived in the climate
of my bedroom windows
punched and filmed by rain
until I saw those kids

and yellow contrails
fuming above their heads
where storm clouds rolled
the time you and I
lunched on Windy Hill,
tuna sandwiches, mustard
flowers in your hair,
a cloudburst that broke us up.

(I'm remembering
the night a downpour's
martial cadence rapped
the skylight above the bed,
how we lived in the instant
and the all at once,
and I lost your words
in our uncertain surround.)

During the storm break,
sulfur flukes rose
over the children's heads
and happy pictures,
a new storm coming,
our half-remembered
half-invented time,
thunder breaking inside
our ears.
    So much
we've known together,
telling stories which
make us believe
as we want to believe
that one thing has to do
with any other
dim ecstatic thing.

More Rain

Red, hard-shelled berry clusters
smothered shrubs and crazed brush
I saw from a bridge above the creek.
My two weeks in the woods
to get away from you, from us.
I went down the wet bank to cut
a bouquet of berries that I found
were ladybugs, hundreds of them,
each shell case bulbing more.
I wanted to share that sight with you.
I even planned how I'd tell it,
happy you couldn't see it when I did.

Same day. Same frame. Small trees
stood midstream in mounds scooped
from feeble banks by recent storms
when the water overcame
its narrow channel. Its force
tore screwy tracks deeper and wider
until those skinny trees bobbed loose.
Same thought. How I'd shape words
to fit that becalmed rich feeling
of extremity. Another story
brought back alive to tell you
or not, if I see you again.

THREE

Driving to Provincetown

"So where *is* Poussin in America, anyway?"
    "There it is. That's him."
Our windows runny with parkway foliage
    while a road crew pours tarmac
across the meridian, black roller aghast
    with summer's steaming workers
vapored in half sun, their mock orange vests
    like the weepy sunset starting
behind the slickered yellow cab. The pharaoh
    sent them to construct
this high road to the sea. Not knowing
    any other way or world,
they pause a moment at the forge of their work
    while the dump truck chutes asphalt
before the roller that rolls on all alike.
    Some are waving their arms,
or red flags or stop signs, doubled
    in the dust of Egypt's desire.

At Mission San Javier

—for Alison Hawthorne Deming

The arroyos flooded, the river ran
so high it nearly touched the bridge;
we stood there with those who came
to watch the water. The red torrent
flowered at the feet of villagers
bunched at the far end, where,
at Easter, their Conquistador Society
will ride down from these desert hills,
shaking earth of its dust,
and run down panicked Indians.

Inside the mission church,
raindrops from your hair
sparked the candlelight.
The walleyed angel in its niche
looked at us and looked away
to its sanctuary sibling who fluffed
a red-checked taffeta petticoat.
The last we saw, before we left
to cross back over that sinking bridge,
sat on a fool-the-eye scallop shell.
Bloody fishnets mantled her shoulders.

The Bull-Roarers

Young men in an Australian tribe are seized by masked
men, carried far from their familiar surroundings, laid
on the ground, and covered with branches. For the first
time they face an absolute darkness made terrifying by
the approach of divinity announced by the bull-roarers.

—*Mircea Eliade*

They come for me when it gets dark.
Large and silent, wearing mummers' masks,
badger claws chinging at their waists,
orange street cones on their heads
like party hats, tied with gut.
They lift and carry me from bed
to a field by our red movie-house,
to bury me in the pit they've primed.
The stars rub their great noise on me.
I think: *I have my own things to bury*
before it gets too late. Herewith, first,
I bury anger, may its sparky pus
not touch my lips again hardly ever.

Second, into the pit I send greed,
may it choke on its ashen, hairy tongue.
Go down, you too, covetousness,
and lick the earth's dungy scabs.
But for myself I keep the following:

Lust, my favorite panic. Charity
for my friends and a few exceptions.
Desire, because what else is there
when warm chestnuts split their skins?
Last, I keep willfulness,
to shoot my mouth off as I please,
even when the roaring buries me
and dirt crawls ear to throat to tongue.

Hermes: Port Authority:
His Song

Hey, mister, find your bus for you?
I burn my tracks, I stink,
I lay down in the dust.
Pardon me, I meant lie. Make time.
Try restrooms, bathrooms, toilets.
Read *Time,* the *Voice* or *Times.*
Nobody believes the subway bombs,
landlords planting land mines
in tunnels where I live
and lay me down to sleep at night.
Show you to your bus
or an excellent candy bar?
A dollar's good. A quarter, too.
Any bus will do.
We got them all. There's Teaneck,
the Oranges and Hackensack,
Atlantic City, too,
those gonads and gourmets,
Robert Goulet and Edie Gourmet.
I'll sell you pussy, nookie,
what you will. I'll soap
your goodies in the men's room sink.
O play me how you will.
Sleep tight. God speed your bus.
A dollar, quarter, dime will do.

Off His Medication This Morning in the Laundromat He Says

This just in
Brownsville Texas
a sleepy border town
struck by another
tragic occurrence
an eleven-year-old boy
angry at school counselors
shot and killed
two innocents lie
in the schoolyard Howard
what's going on today
at the White House
with denials all around
and in a world that doesn't
believe in royalty
she was everybody's princess
today's best buy
strawberries and green beans
we've just learned
a bus carrying teenagers
from a soccer match
they had just won
foggy and cool
clearing in the p.m.
and so back to you.

50

Tambourine Action

What flavored pain in your
Small change or smaller?

ticky surplus flannels
gutter-punk pals and buck-

toothed boyfriend hooting
Dollar for a Guinness?

Sing *Anybody?* to your lab pup
on a rope under stemware

and vinyl chaps in windows
smiling up *Yoo-hoo*

from your sticky poverties
to catch my eye.

Today you're hiding what?
I'll make up stories

for your pain and they
will serve you right.

You're from a suburb
of cars growing in garages

and sun on dogwood egg-
shell shadows on the ground.

Or Daddy hit you and Mom cried
you hated Fresno anyway

the meds did you no good
but here you've met your man

and ask no pity for true love
that now asks for so much.

Girl with Pearl Earring
by Johannes Vermeer

He put the spirit essence
the light pip not only
in each eye's albumen
concentrate of starlight
but must have been taught
how to do that by first
finding it in the pearl
he posed then corrected
in dusty studio light
that pounced on the window
behind which sits the cheeky girl
pear- and apple-blossom cheeks
a fake description naturally
of their plain fleshiness
drably golden and her lips
from Haight Street's darlings
nose studs jacket studs
girls with that kind of eye
one by the ATM machine
casual juicy and so fair
a Netherlandish type
panhandling strangers
pomegranate-seed ball
bearings agleam in her nose

pearls not sea-harvested
but imagined seen put there
by a certain need and fancy
because love says it's so
picture that picture this.

Stanzas

At the Cole and Carl dog-run park,
mutts and poodles sniff grass,
couples laugh, the N-Judah
sharks from its tunnel. I'm druggy
while my doctor fools with dosages
to stagger my soul's bad chemistry.

I need a looser world and words for it.
Last night I watched the Dog Star burn
blue then frosted mercury. *Late Show*
station break, I write lines like these,
looking for exacter, plainer poetry
while more stars appear. I hate mornings—

my bed's a mudlake writing pulls me from.
Poetry's muscled homemade demon
sits on me and asks: "What next?"
A mockingbird sings from its nest,
dark or light the same, singing
end to end, while the kitchen light

curls me over short, easy books,
dumped crosswords, and *Vanity Fair.*
Then life's casual rush stops,
everywhere I look
the lymph in things goes dead,
though the world still shines the same.

Medicated to this willowed balance,
I don't weep now to see dogs run
or wild fennel bend to winds
kiting a tern from its brilliant marsh.
I don't get sick with fright to hear
an eyelash click across the street.

Little lab-rat gods rattling
in my jar, keep me close enough
to smell dog fur and fresh-cut grass.
Take away whatever you want,
but deliver me to derangements
of sweet, ordered, derelict words.

Add Salt

—for August Kleinzahler

Prometheus lighted a torch at the sun and broke from
it a glowing coal which he thrust into a fennel stalk.

The AMERICAN GNOSTIC CHURCH marquee
fizzes in my window's broken capillaries
caused, the conductor says, by new glass
reacting to the air. I feel fogged in.

Here again are pied scrap-metal cubes
and racked junkers freaked by light,
and here I am again trying to say
what I see. It makes me hungrier.

The horse track's floating island,
the English Language Institute,
car wash, tar-shingle roofs,
U-rent lockers, and tap-rooms.

Same commute, same things in their orders
briefing past my view. Still looking
for the invisible life of things,
I can't get beyond or into amassings

and breaks of matter, green clabber
scumming puddles alongside the train,
then brickyards banked on body shops,
homeless trackside nappers under trees,

ditchwater where shopping carts come to drink,
where wild fennel thrives, as in Sicily,
to receive yellow embers our hero stole
to crown the graygreen stalk.

Its lacy tops I'll toss with macaroni
and fresh sardines from Monterey—
licorice feathers, movie-houses, anisette
women served men on holy days,
                 Pernod, too,
white like my window, or a Sazerac
greened with absinthe, O how it bends
yes to wind wash and bayshore gusts.
Next stop I'll step off and pick a bunch,

boil a pot of water in the aisle,
blow the sullen coals alive,
and invite the regulars and pony players,
my place at eight, we can talk over dinner.

Kindness on Via del Cuccolo

The bachelor farmer she rented from offered this and that.
Eggs, pepper braids, oil, a chine of ham he cured himself.
She said no, thank you, a few eggs maybe, that's already
too much. Next month he offered more, she said no again.
Where does it stop? Widowed young, renting country-cheap,
she could have, he swore, anything she wants.
Dried figs, fiery banana fruit, or half a pig.
"Where would I put it?" she said, kind and noncommittal.
"I'll keep it for you. Come anytime, take what you need."
Why not make use of him as he would make of her?

Late-spring afternoon. The cuckoo sang upon the lane.
Her lover Massimo jagged his plangent Deux Chevaux
down mud furrows. Poplar seeds flurried everywhere.
He wept in the kitchen, because his young son stole
small change from Mama's purse, to pay him
not to leave. At least that's what Mama said.
She kindly gave him food and waited more for him
while he waited to leave his son. Love kept her in love.
The cuckoo sang all afternoon. Too soon. Too soon.
Fresh love, basket of fresh eggs, and an open purse.

Tuxedo, New York

Wind on the water and green things
on that water. The lakeside woman
puts the colors from her hands
upon the lake that's coming into life
under her hands, while birds call
and cry through shaking oaks above
the dragonflies, green dragonflies,
kissing tips of reeds, motes,
water lilies, whatever sits in the scene.
She looks out and paints the scene
while voices from branches across the lake
flee through the cedars to stop
at the water restless on her easel.
Yellow jackets change the air
around her head. Her paper hat
flies in the wind. Water bugs draw
circles around lily pads and nothing
is apart from any other thing.
The bullfrogs make their bronzed noise,
then motorboats afflict that noise,
flesh appears on far white banks
while the woman at her colors watches,
moves her brush and finger as if it's she
changing for real the sky's face
moving on the water, the pictured water
that doesn't stir, or live, and is our life.

South End

The Judas tree down there peeling red
beside the flowering dogwood,
a late-May sky covering our terrace,
that birch lit from within, scent of roses
somewhere in the park below,
and aren't those gardenias?
Taking it all in.
It's not May, it's March,
too early for everything,
and there's a small woman
or large girl snow-writing
LOVE U CHR.
We look for signs left
roughly for our concern.
Other meanings hang
in March ice in trees,
sparrows and squirrels, no leaves,
snowdirt bumps melting around
iron lampposts that light the scene
for us. Writing the season,
we taste whatever we choose to see,
rocket and lettuce of a summer night
we don't yet know and won't forget,
the garden green and snowy,
pansies finally coming in
where this winter message was.

Rainy Night After
Christmas Party

A mackerel sky already shaking rain
that bucks against my high window

where in better weather I'll see past my face
to bridge towers horned against the headlands,

the radio fork's methodical red lights
and strong signals, but Glenn Gould,

moaning a partita in the glass,
fades out to the hills and Farallons.

I scrape the dinner dishes while my friends
who laughed here over lettuce an hour ago

turn back a flannel sheet, feel its fall
on tougher flannelly skin, ankle and thigh,

breaths triggered by snickers and oohs,
soaped minty flesh, shoulder blade, and arm.

In my bed, watching rain pip the windows,
I'll be with those lover guests, their futon,

four-poster, or water bed ribbed when we stir.
They're talking about yesterday's double rainbow

while Kezar's stadium lights shred the window
here where I kissed them all good night,

saw myself ghosted in the nonstop rain
that falls on Kezar's thin nighttime runners

running around the track, vapors running
past pine greens in my bat-wing candlelight.

Police

How oddly quiet
the squad car's light rack
flashing late tonight,
double-parked on my street,
the sea-chilled dark
tweaked by blues and reds,
the old sleepy houses
gap-toothed and aroused
like jack-o'-lanterns,
moments before you phoned
to say the doctors found,
sooner than expected,
new hot spots, metastasized
in her femur, vertebrae,
lung, and brain, making
of course no noise,
your voice how calmly
familiar with whatever's
worse and imaginable
repeating what you said
just weeks ago about
"the geometrical rigor
of retributive forces
in the universe"
while the car throws
its important lights
against the uneventful night.

Duboce Park

Late March and warmer drafts
kicking barefoot children at their kite strings

on grassy onion-dome shadows.
Purple gables, streetlamps,

coy finials and stick facades
legislate the scene.

Kite strings drooping S or U,
our weather and daily measure

of blue sky, sea breeze,
slippages in the atmosphere,

children who reach to a heaven
beyond the buckling lines,

not quite on our ground,
gusting from us while

squinty nannies make crowns
of wisdom braids built of grass.

Higher up, cooler invisible lines
appear to us who think we see,

where kites don't catch the wind
and flesh-haunted emptiness

sketches us to ourselves,
bony, crosshatched, dreamy

for deity or dreaming it,
a heaven that falls and fits

this earth, these house rows, backyards,
the dog paths worn into the grass,

the sandbox and its twisting swings
empty where the children were just now

before they ran behind the kites,
running from us and our feeble facts,

as if another god shouts in their hearts,
scrambled, messier, but loving those

who run through soft grass, looking up
to Bat Signal or dragon bandoneon.

A NOTE ABOUT THE AUTHOR

W. S. Di Piero was born in South Philadelphia in 1945. He is the author of six previous books of poetry, as well as three volumes of translation from the Italian. He writes about art for the *San Diego Reader* and has published three collections of essays and criticism on art, literature and personal experience. His honors include a Guggenheim Fellowship, a National Endowment for the Arts grant and a Lila Wallace–Reader's Digest Writer's Award. He lives in San Francisco and teaches at Stanford University.

A NOTE ON THE TYPE

The text of this book was set in a typeface named Perpetua, designed by the British artist Eric Gill (1882–1940) and cut by the Monotype Corporation of London in 1928–30. Perpetua is a contemporary letter of original design, without any direct historical antecedents. The shapes of the roman letters basically derive from stonecutting, and the italic is essentially an inclined roman. The general effect of the typeface in reading sizes is one of lightness and grace.

Designed and composed by Robert C. Olsson
Printed and bound by Edwards Brothers, Ann Arbor, Michigan